Early Childhood Bulletin Boards

by
Carolyn Wilhelm

boards designed by June Jacobsen

illustrated by Kathryn Hyndman

Cover by Kathryn Hyndman

Shining Star Publications, Copyright © 1987
A Division of Good Apple, Inc.

ISBN No. 0-86653-393-1

Standardized Subject Code TA ac

Printing No. 987

Shining Star Publications
A Division of Good Apple, Inc.
Box 299
Carthage, IL 62321-0299

Unless otherwise indicated, the New International version of the Bible, Children's Edition, was used in preparing the activities in this book.

TO THE TEACHER

This bulletin board book was written for very young learners. Each display encourages the participation of the children in the final creation. You make the caption, and often the children finish the bulletin board.

An easy way to enlarge the illustrations for your specific needs is to use an overhead projector. Trace the patterns found in this book on clear transparency material and then place them on your projector. Now you are ready to make your illustrations as large or as small as you desire. Finally, color, cut and pin the illustrations to the bulletin board.

The table activities were designed to allow children space to play through the new information and stories presented on the bulletin boards. But many of the table activities would work well as lessons without the bulletin board displays.

Scriptures are from the Holy Bible, New International Version, Children's Edition. I used the children's edition because the text matches the regular version, with the added beauty of illustrations. If you have a few minutes to spare in class, students like to look at the pictures in the NIV Children's Edition and pick a story they want read to them. Children will listen to an amazing amount of Scripture in this way, in understandable but beautiful language. "For the word of God is living." Hebrews 4:12

You might want to take photos of each child in your class at the beginning of the year for use on the bulletin boards. Pin the appropriate photo near the artwork done by each child. Small children cannot read each others' names, but can easily identify classmates' work when their photographs are attached near their work. Parents will enjoy this also. Everyone becomes a star, and children love this extra, positive reinforcement.

Now, on to class . . . see if your curriculum could benefit from this unique collection of bulletin boards and table displays. Study the lessons and "teach them to your children." Deuteronomy 4:9

In Christ,

Carolyn Wilhelm

DEDICATED TO

Gary, Michael and Betsy.
c.w.

Garret, Dane, Tague, Chad and Cory.
j.j.

Shining Star Publications, Copyright © 1987, A division of Good Apple, Inc.   SS182

TABLE OF CONTENTS

A Whale of a Tale 5
A Garden of Verses 7
Sonbeaming 8
Joy 9
Press On 10
Let the Little Children Come to Me 11
"Ark" You Glad for Animals? 12
This Train Is Bound for Glory! 13
Basket Baby Moses 14
Trust in Us 15
Looking for Verses 16
Rock of Ages 17
Fishers of Men 18
And What Does the Lord Require of You? 19
In God We Trust 21
My Burden Is Light 23
Celebrate! 24
He's True Blue 25
The Lord Our God Will Call 26
On the Wings of a Dove 27
Peace Pieces 29
Hide 'n Seek? 30
Don't Be Sheepish! 31
God May Be All in All 32
Newsworthy Notes 33
A Spirit of Power 35
Learn Your Lessons Well! 36
Aim for Perfection 37
Love, Love, Love 39
Rejoicing! Rooms 40
Who Will Be My Friend? 41
Marvelous Medicine! 43
The Mustard Seed 45
Footprints 46
And the Walls Come a Tumblin' Down 47
You Are the Salt of the Earth! 48
Down in My Heart 49
Open, Open 51
Happy Birthday, Jesus! 53
Obey Bay 54
Helpers in Our Church 55
You Must Not Eat from the Tree 56
Hairy Heads! 57
Praise Him with the Strings and Flute 58
Play and Verse Match 59

Shining Star Publications, Copyright © 1987, A division of Good Apple, Inc.

SS1825

A Forest of Verses 61
At the End of Our Rainbow 63
Knock, Knock, Who's There? 64
Time to Trust 65
Noise and Rejoice! 67
Star Splendor 68
Who Is . . . the Greatest 69
New Nets 70
Silver and Gold 71
Apples of Gold 72
Watch Us Grow 73
It's Planting Time! 75
Bearing Banners 76
Silent Secrets 77
Fleet Feet 78
Unique! 79
Forget Me Not 80
His Heart Is Steadfast 81
Our Happy Year 82
Seeds of Good Deeds 83
Finding a Book in the Bible 85
Pure and Lovely Thoughts 87
The Church Is People! 88
God Is Love and from Above 89
My "Rock" Collection 90
Rule by Rule 91
God's Greatest Gift to Us 92
Award Certificates 93

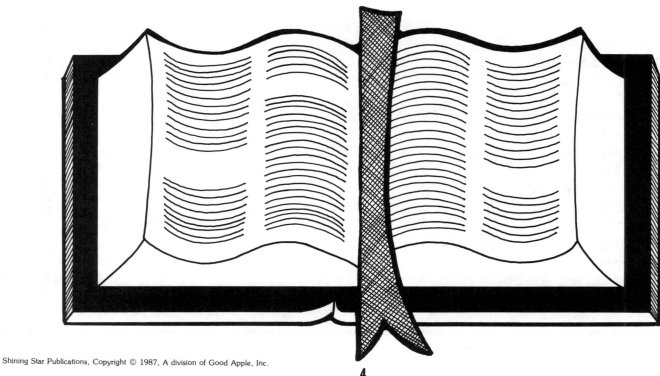

"SALVATION COMES FROM THE LORD." Jonah 2:9

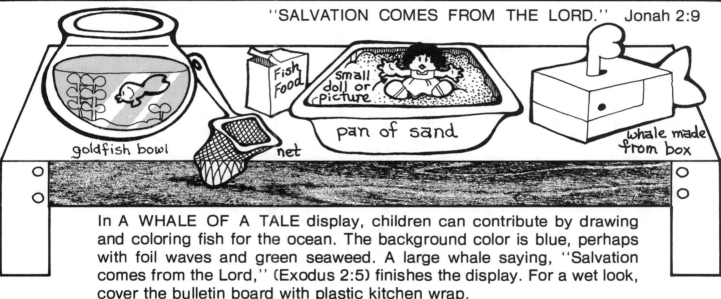

In A WHALE OF A TALE display, children can contribute by drawing and coloring fish for the ocean. The background color is blue, perhaps with foil waves and green seaweed. A large whale saying, "Salvation comes from the Lord," (Exodus 2:5) finishes the display. For a wet look, cover the bulletin board with plastic kitchen wrap.

The hands-on activity table might include a goldfish for the class to care for, a pan of sand for Jonah to recover in and a whale made out of a cereal box so the whale can "swallow" Jonah as the children reenact the story. Some children may share a whale or fish stuffed-animal toy, or other related items.

EXTENDED ACTIVITIES: Add pictures (from Sunday School leaflets or old bulletins) of other "whales" of tales. The similarity of theme that salvation comes from the LORD should be noted. Items for these other stories could be added to the table for story play by the children.

Children may enjoy making whales and Jonahs for take-home projects. A cereal box cut and painted black makes a good puppet whale. Jonah may be drawn free-hand or colored from a Xerox sheet. (See pattern on the following page.)

SS1825

A WHALE OF A TALE
(Patterns)

JONAH

WHALE SPOUT

WHALE EYES

WHALE TAIL

fold back

fold back

fold back

fold back

SS1825

"LEARN YOUR DECREES." Psalm 119:71

This A GARDEN OF VERSES display could be left up an entire season. Plastic flowers, pictures of animals, paper, garden tools and small index cards with the children's verses from the lessons could be pinned up to the display. Each Sunday, students could draw stars on their cards to show which verses they have memorized.

All the verses for the season could be displayed at the beginning of the year, or each Sunday one verse could be added. Each Sunday, all verses to date could be reviewed.

EXTENDED ACTIVITY: Send home a verse sheet, such as the one below. Parents could check daily on the verse of the week, and make a check mark the day the student memorizes all of the verse.

	Mon.	Tues.	Wed.	Thur.	Fri.	Sat.	
VERSE 1							
VERSE 2							
VERSE 3							
VERSE 4							

...ications, Copyright © 1987, A division of Good Apple, Inc. SS1825

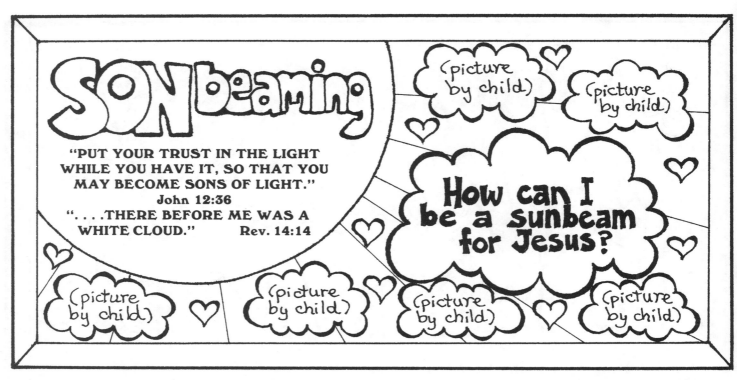

"THE RIGHTEOUS WILL SHINE LIKE THE SUN." Matthew 13:43

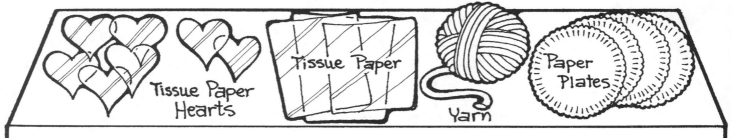

SONBEAMING will give the children time to think about how they might be sunbeams for Jesus. Let the children draw their pictures on scattered clouds—emphasizing that the sunshine also comes through clouds. When the children are sunbeams for Jesus, His love shines through them. Display the cloud pictures on the bulletin board. Write sentences on the pictures to explain the children's ideas.

TABLE ACTIVITY: Place paper plates with the centers cut out, tissue paper, tissue paper hearts, and yarn bows on the table for the children. Print "God's love shines through us" on each plate. The children can make paper plates that the sun will shine through when they hang in the window. In the hole in the paper plate, tissue paper is glued (on the back) and a tissue paper heart is pasted lightly on that. The sunshine comes through the tissue paper and heart, as God's love shines through us.

HANG
WIN

"YOU WOULD ALL SHARE MY JOY."
II Corinthians 2:3

"ALWAYS PRAY WITH JOY."
Philippians 1:4

JOY is spelled by children forming the letters. Students could spell out J-O-Y by using floor space and creative ideas. Other words that could be spelled out by an average-sized group include: JOY, PEACE, HOPE, LOVE.

EXTENDED ACTIVITY: Take photos of children forming words to add to this display—other words they have thought of. What a way to learn to spell!

SS1825

(Pictures of students' families biking, swimming, hiking, etc.)

"GOD IS OUR REFUGE AND STRENGTH." Psalm 46:1

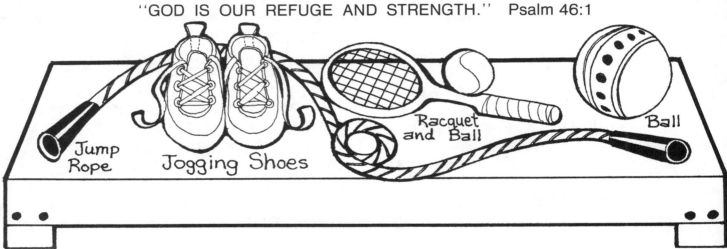

Jump Rope

Jogging Shoes

Racquet and Ball

Ball

Ask church members to contribute pictures of their families in action in activities such as jogging, biking, swimming, and so on. Use these for a display captioned, PRESS ON . . . KEEP THE FAITH! A table with some gym supplies could be put under the display during an occasion such as Vacation Bible School, where there would be opportunity for such activities for the children.

EXTENDED ACTIVITY: Include a Bible Olympics with "races" for learning a verse, song, or prayer and with small ribbons for coming in first, second, or for participating. Students in upper grades might help plan such an event. Tables might be set up with verses to unscramble to aid memorization, where a song could be learned, where students put the books of the Bible on index cards in order, and so on.

"I HAVE FOUGHT THE GOOD FIGHT, I HAVE FINISHED THE RACE, I HAVE KEPT THE FAITH." II Timothy 4:7

"FOR PHYSICAL TRAINING IS OF SOME VALUE, BUT GODLINESS HAS VALUE FOR ALL THINGS." I Timothy 4:8

SS1825

LET THE LITTLE CHILDREN COME TO ME is the caption for a display to which children could add photos of themselves. These photos could be ones such as school pictures or any others. Drawings the children have made of themselves could also be used.

On the table below the display, you might want to display a set of hand-prints in the position of praying (hands together on the side). On this paper could be added prayers the children have used in Sunday school. A few pictures of children praying could also be added.

EXTENDED ACTIVITY: Encourage children to have parents and other family members make praying hands prints and add their favorite prayers to the page. Display all these for everyone to enjoy.

SS1825

"ARK" You Glad for Animals?

"AND NOAH DID ALL THAT THE LORD COMMANDED HIM." Genesis 7:5

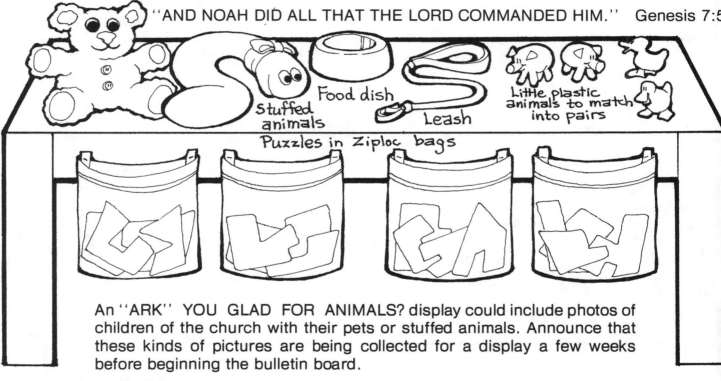

Stuffed animals

Food dish

Leash

Little plastic animals to match into pairs

Puzzles in Ziploc bags

An "ARK" YOU GLAD FOR ANIMALS? display could include photos of children of the church with their pets or stuffed animals. Announce that these kinds of pictures are being collected for a display a few weeks before beginning the bulletin board.

Puzzles may be placed on the table and could include several pictures of animals on index cards, cut into two parts, and then placed in Ziploc bags with several animals in each bag.

The tabletop could also have a few stuffed animals, food dishes for animals, a leash, and a box of small plastic animals the children could try to match into pairs or groups. Items could be loaned by individual families.

We care for animals as we care for others, with love.

"LOVE ONE ANOTHER. AS I HAVE LOVED YOU, SO YOU MUST LOVE ONE ANOTHER." John 13:34

EXTENDED ACTIVITY: Have a pet show.

SS1825

THIS TRAIN IS BOUND FOR GLORY!

"LEARN TO DO RIGHT!" Isaiah 1:17

The THIS TRAIN IS BOUND FOR GLORY! display uses boxes (such as cereal boxes) tacked to the bulletin board to hold church items such as a hymnal, a Bible, a bulletin, and some pictures of people doing kind deeds. A rainbow, the sun and clouds are the background for the "train" of paper-covered boxes. During Sunday School the teacher can pull the items needed for the lesson out of the display. Perhaps the leaflet or Sunday School activity page could be put in one box.

The table items may include the same items as in the display for students to look at themselves. Pictures of people doing kind deeds may be glued onto tagboard, cut as puzzle pieces and put in Ziploc bags for a student activity.

EXTENDED ACTIVITY: Have a magnetic toy train for the table display. On the sides of the train where the cars connect, small happy faces could be taped showing how people in a church community "connect."

> "BUT IF WE WALK IN THE LIGHT, AS HE IS THE LIGHT, WE HAVE
> FELLOWSHIP WITH ONE ANOTHER."   I John 1:7

On the cars might be taped small pictures of people doing kind things, or such pictures could be taped to a construction paper "track" on the table.

The class could consider a special project, such as taking favors for the lunch trays to a nursing home, or some other concerted sharing of love.

> "GOD IS LIGHT. IN HIM THERE IS NO DARKNESS AT ALL."
>   I John 1:5

SS1825

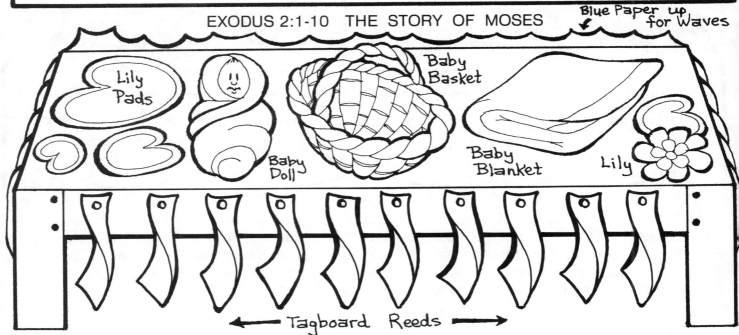

EXODUS 2:1-10   THE STORY OF MOSES

BASKET BABY MOSES naturally accompanies a lesson for young children about baby Moses. A blue background with foil cut as waves and a lightweight baby blanket set the stage for a very light stuffed baby doll or picture of a baby.

The table can be decorated as the river, complete with green streamers for reeds. Blue paper on the table would look like water. A few students might like to color ''lily pads.'' A baby basket, baby doll and blanket would complete the table. Then students could reenact the story with friends in class. (One could hide under the table, and so on.)

EXTENDED ACTIVITY: Students might want to act out the story for another class, with the table as a prop and partial stage.

''SHE SAW THE BASKET AMONG THE REEDS AND SENT HER SLAVE
   GIRL TO GET IT.''
                                                           Exodus 2:5

SS1825

TRUST IN US . . . DON'T LET YOUR CHRISTIANITY RUST! Materials for this display include the caption and large pictures of Jesus, the Bible, a cross, etc. An OPTIONAL TABLE ACTIVITY might include some rusted items in jars (so they are not dangerous) and an older pan or baking sheet that looks terrible. These would aid understanding of the idea of ''rust'' and serve as discussion starters.

EXTENDED ACTIVITY: Have the students think up some ''commercials'' to tape record to help others avoid ''rusting.'' Anti-drugs, anti-alcoholism, and other ideas from television would help students be able to think of similar commercials. The students would enjoy hearing their tapes played back.

SS1825

LOOKING FOR VERSES begins with children drawing eyes and cutting them out to attach to the display. The caption and mirror are prepared by the teacher. Children can practice cheerful looks into the pretend mirror, into mirrors on the table and for others.

TABLE ACTIVITY: Look into a mirror and draw a picture of what you see.

EXTENDED ACTIVITY: Have a "mirror walk." Children look into mirrors for guidance on where to walk.

"LOOK TO THE LORD."   Psalm 105:4

"THE LORD HAS DONE THIS, AND IT IS MARVELOUS IN
OUR EYES."   Matthew 21:42

"THE EYES OF THE LORD ARE ON THE RIGHTEOUS."
Psalm 34:15

SS1825

ROCK OF AGES

"HE is my rock." Ps. 92:15

Modern Person

Biblical Person

Settler

Space Person

Pilgrim

Sunday School Class

David Copperfield Type

Settler

Pilgrim

Modern Person

"KING OF THE AGES."
Revelation 15:3

ROCK OF AGES is intended to show the young learner how God has been a "rock" for people of all times. Pictures of people from different times will help children begin to understand the concept. A cross on the rock will help them realize that the rock is Christ.

EXTENDED ACTIVITY: Have students bring rocks to class, with verses tied onto them. These rocks can be displayed and then sent home when the display is taken down. The young learners will like hunting for rocks, and the verses will also become more memorable.

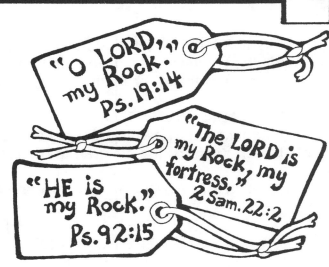

"O LORD," my Rock. Ps. 19:14

"The LORD is my Rock, my fortress." 2 Sam. 22:2

"HE is my Rock." Ps. 92:15

SS1825

FISHERS OF MEN is an action-centered display for which children make the fish and tell the teacher what to write on them. The children think up ideas of how to ''fish'' for people for Jesus, or to show they've been ''caught.''

The TABLE ACTIVITY is a magnet game with a fishing pole that ''catches'' fish by magnetism between the magnet and a paper clip. On the table are fish, with ideas written on them for the children to do to be ''fishers'' of men.

EXTENDED ACTIVITY: Encourage the children to do kind deeds for others.

''IN THE SAME WAY, LET YOUR LIGHT SHINE BEFORE MEN, THAT THEY MAY SEE YOUR GOOD DEEDS AND PRAISE YOUR FATHER IN HEAVEN.''
Matthew 5:16

SS1825

AND WHAT DOES THE LORD REQUIRE OF YOU? The children will be actively involved in making this bulletin board. The smiling face portion is for pictures from magazines, pictures drawn by the children, or words telling how the children might act justly and love mercy. The sad face side might show pictures of fighting, etc.

The TABLE ACTIVITY involves children in more action by having them make their own puppets. They can act out how they might act as grown-ups, do difficult things such as share, and so on. The puppets, described on the next page, are made from large business-sized white envelopes.

SS1825

AND WHAT DOES THE LORD REQUIRE OF YOU ACTIVITY PAGE

Envelope Puppets

Materials needed: Business-size white envelopes
                            scissors
                            crayons
(optional)   buttons/snaps for eyes, odds and ends for hair and clothes.

1. Lick envelopes and seal. Cut off one end.

(Hand will go in here.)

2. Cut out armholes for fingers to go through.

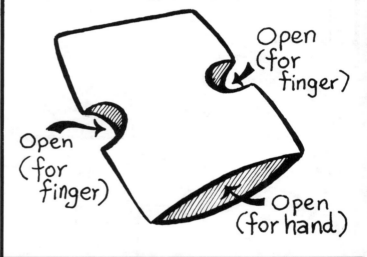

Open (for finger)

Open (for finger)

Open (for hand)

3. Decorate!

4. Use!

SS1825

"I TRUST IN THE LORD." Psalm 31:6

IN GOD WE TRUST could begin with students doing coin rubbings on lightweight paper or aluminum foil. Have them find the words "In God We Trust." Then they could create "Christian coins." Using one of the verses and an idea for illustrating it, they could create coins for display. (See patterns on the following page.)

A discussion could be held about the new money:
    What is your money worth?
    What would it buy?
    What would it help our church do?
    Would only good things happen with this money?
    Which coins look like real money?
    Which look like they wouldn't ever be used like real money?
    Should we all change to these new coins?
    Do we already have Christian coins?

Shining Star Publications, Copyright © 1987, A division of Good Apple, Inc.

SS1825

IN GOD WE TRUST . . .
(Patterns)

SS1825

MY BURDEN IS LIGHT is to help children understand that their burdens or worries can be given up to Christ. Rest can be found from the earthly problems even children face, with faith in God.

TABLE ACTIVITY: Use "Gentle Graffiti" for this activity. The children may draw things they can do when they are very worried . . . they may draw themselves praying alone or in groups, singing, going to church, reading or just holding a Bible. The group might share some worries, and the teacher could pray with the children about these things.

SS1825

A day with any treat as part of the lesson can be used with this CELEBRATE display. Musical notes, streamers, stars with sequins, circles cut into spirals, and yarn bows might be pinned up with the verses.

This bulletin board might be coordinated with a church celebration or even a special fellowship time . . . or when students bake cookies for a Bible School program.

EXTENDED ACTIVITY: Bake cookies or make no-bake cookies; or mix and stir punch. The party might be transported to a nursing home.

SS1825

"THE LORD IS RIGHT AND TRUE." Psalm 33:4

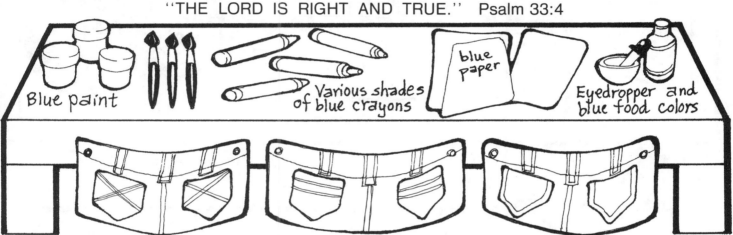

Blue paint · Various shades of blue crayons · blue paper · Eyedropper and blue food colors

HE'S TRUE BLUE . . . CAN YOU BE, TOO? begins with blue . . . blue crayons, blue paint, blue water color. Add blue jeans pockets that have "true blue" verses in them. Students can experiment with blue art and discuss the term "true blue." They might look in the mirror on the Bible Board to see if they reflect hearts that are true. This display is made with large blue tagboard cutouts to look like blue crayons, paint and a heart.

EXTENDED ACTIVITY: Have students wear blue jeans for a Sunday School session or church activity evening. Each student might receive a verse to put into a pocket. Upon some signal—like a song or a bell ringing—each student must take out the verse, read it for a friend, and exchange verses. For the very young, all can have the same verse so the repetition of saying it upon the signal will help them with memorization.

First graders might write a verse inside a "crayon" holder. (See illustration.)

SS1825

Children may have heard people say they were called by God. This display will help them relate to this idea. The caption THE LORD OUR GOD WILL CALL is illustrated with a large paper phone. Does God really use a telephone?

TABLE ACTIVITY: Use toy phones to dramatize being ''called'' by God. What things might people be called to do? How would students respond?

The message pad and pencils would be fun for the children.

SS1825

"A CHEERFUL HEART IS GOOD MEDICINE." Proverbs 17:22
"THE CHILD GREW AND BECAME STRONG IN SPIRIT."
Luke 1:80

ON THE WINGS OF A DOVE, the Spirit, our thoughts can go heavenward. This display needs a caption and the dove (pattern page follows). On their doves the children can draw uplifting thoughts (things that make them happy when they are feeling sad).

The doves, when finished, could be shared in a circle discussion before being displayed for all to see.

EXTENDED ACTIVITY: Have a table set up with heavy items and light items in different boxes. Drop the two different weight items. Which falls the faster? Do they fall at the same speed? Why do heavy worries and thoughts weigh you down? Why do light and happy thoughts lift you up? As a follow-up game, mix all the objects in one pile and let the children sort them.

"TAKE MY YOKE UPON YOU AND LEARN FROM ME, FOR I AM GENTLE AND HUMBLE IN HEART, AND YOU WILL FIND REST FOR YOUR SOULS. FOR MY YOKE IS EASY AND MY BURDEN IS LIGHT."
Matthew 11:29-30

SS1825

ON THE WINGS OF A DOVE . . .
(Pattern)

SS1825

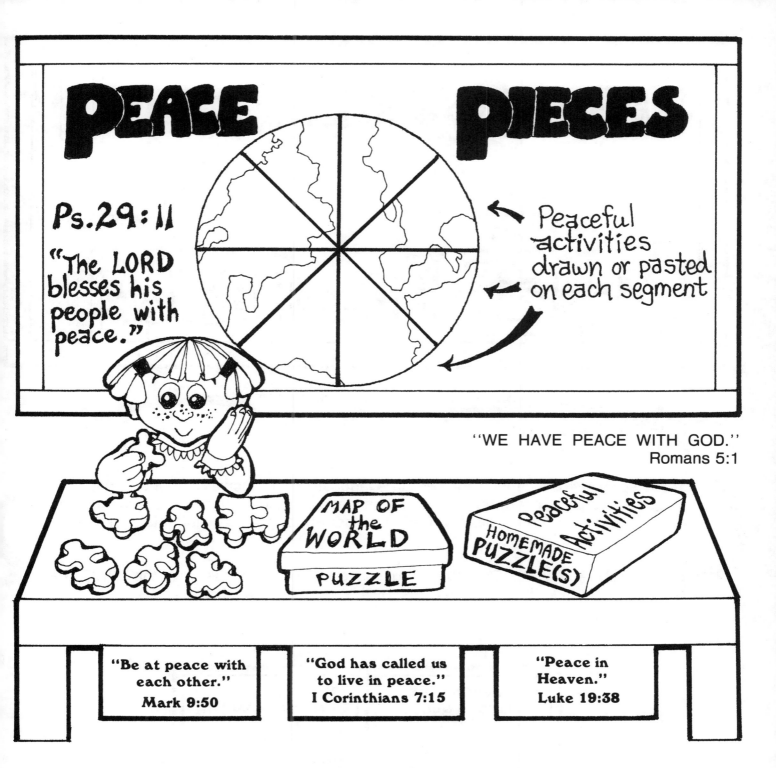

PEACE PIECES needs a caption and one or two world maps cut into circles. Cut the maps into triangles as for pizza, and for each piece let students draw or cut and paste magazine pictures of peaceful activities for God's people.

The TABLE ACTIVITY includes simply a puzzle of the world or the United States, whichever is available. A homemade puzzle of a peaceful activity could be put out also. This may be made by gluing a poster onto cardboard and cutting into pieces.

EXTENDED ACTIVITY: Have children think of a peaceful project for church or community and then carry it out. Visiting a nursing home, helping out at a church function or even cleaning the church supply closet might be a place to start.

SS1825

"SEEK THE LORD." Deuteronomy 4:29

HIDE 'N SEEK? NO!
  SEEK BUT DON'T HIDE!

This display needs a caption and two large tagboard items such as a door (see page 52) and a large chair. Children's faces could be made to "peek" from behind the door and chair to help illustrate the display. Perhaps older Sunday School students could create this display for a younger class.

EXTENDED ACTIVITY: On small cards have verses about seeking the Lord. The teacher would hide these before class for the students to seek and find.

Verses for the small cards could include

SS1825

Don't Be Sheepish! Be a Lamb of God!

"MY PEOPLE HAVE BEEN LOST SHEEP." Jeremiah 50:6

DON'T BE SHEEPISH! BE A LAMB OF GOD! is the caption on this bulletin board along with a large cardboard shape of a lamb. Students can add cotton balls to cover the lamb, and write their names on circles to pin on cotton balls. The lamb can be a class project.

TABLE ACTIVITY: Have lambs made individually by students using just a few cotton balls. Add a foil "lake." Students can dramatize Bible stories with their lambs.

EXTENDED ACTIVITY: Include dramatization of the lost sheep stories or pantomimes of how people can be lambs of God.

"The lamb is its lamp." Rev. 21:23

"I am sending you out like lambs." Luke 10:3

CIRCLE WITH NAME TO PIN COTTON BALL ONTO SHEEP DRAWING ON BULLETIN BOARD

SS1825

God May Be All in All.
1 Cor. 15:28

Jesus takes care of the world.

"FOR HE HAS PUT EVERYTHING UNDER HIS FEET."
I Corinthians 15:27

WORLD MAP

Cut out world continents from map; place on sand

GOD MAY BE ALL IN ALL (I Corinthians 15:28) by putting everything under the feet of Jesus. A dark blue background, the planet Earth, stars and planets go under the large feet of Jesus, to complete this bulletin board.

TABLE ACTIVITY: Children can make footprints by pressing an old pair of sandals into a tray of sand. A cut-up world map can be put in the sand. Church missions might be identified with stars placed on a large world map.

SS1825

The entire congregation can be involved in displaying NEWSWORTHY NOTES. Using the existing caption, the bird patterns (see pattern on the following page), paper voice balloons, and pens, church members can post current ''good news'' items that affect the young students. The children can color the birds, while parents or friends print the messages for the voice balloons.

Church events may also be posted on this bulletin board.

Shining Star Publications, Copyright © 1987, A division of Good Apple, Inc.

SS1825

NEWSWORTHY
NOTES
(Pattern)

SS1825

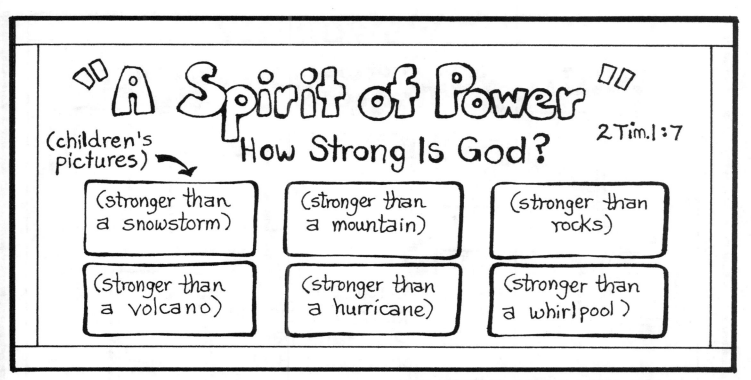

"A Spirit of Power"

(children's pictures)→

How Strong Is God?

2 Tim. 1:7

(stronger than a snowstorm)

(stronger than a mountain)

(stronger than rocks)

(stronger than a volcano)

(stronger than a hurricane)

(stronger than a whirlpool)

"PROCLAIM THE POWER OF GOD."
Psalm 68:34

"BE STRONG IN THE LORD AND IN HIS MIGHTY POWER."
Ephesians 6:10

HYMNS for Children

SONGS

"The LORD is my strength and my song."
Is. 12:2

SONG BOOK

SONG BOOK

SONG BOOK

"GOD is the strength of my heart."
Ps. 73:26

A SPIRIT OF POWER will let the children consider the question "How strong is God?" and lets them answer with pictorial representations of their ideas. The teacher writes a sentence or phrase explaining the idea of each picture.

TABLE ACTIVITY: Learn a verse:
        "THE LORD IS MY STRENGTH AND MY SONG."   Isaiah 12:2

Take time to explore song books for other appropriate songs about this topic.

SS1825

This bulletin board LEARN YOUR LESSONS WELL! uses photos taken at church gatherings or at Sunday School.

Pictures from long ago and the present can be used. A picture of an older church member as a young Sunday School student would show the value of learning lessons well.

TABLE ACTIVITY: The table display could include familiar church items, leaflets, Bibles, paper, crayons and other Sunday School materials.

EXTENDED ACTIVITY: In a circle discussion the students take turns sharing the lessons they have learned and that have been the most valuable to them.

SS1825

The AIM FOR PERFECTION . . . LISTEN! bulletin board will help students focus on good listening skills.

TABLE ACTIVITY: Students who listen will receive awards for their good efforts. The teacher can make out the certificates and "mail" them to the students by taping them to the table for pickup the next week. (See the awards on the following page and additional awards on pages 93-96.)

SS1825

LISTENING AWARD

Lovely Listening

You were all ears during Sunday School!

"At the Lord's feet listening to what He said."
Luke 10:39

To:_____
From:_____

Church:_____

LISTENING AWARD

Great Listening!

You were so attentive during Sunday School!

"Let the Wise Listen."
Prov. 1:5

To:_____
From:_____

Church:_____

SS1825

LOVE, LOVE, LOVE is the caption on this bulletin board. A large paper heart with the picture of a child wearing a crown of hearts is displayed. The five verses above may be printed on 9″ × 12″ paper and displayed. Children have heard that loving Jesus helps make them likeable, and the verse shown above, John 14:21, may help children understand this concept.

TABLE ACTIVITY: Have materials to make crowns of love: tagboard strips 24″ long, hearts or heart patterns, paper and markers. The teacher writes verses on the crown materials ahead of time. The children can make heart necklaces with the words of John 14:21 printed on them.

EXTENDED ACTIVITY: While children are sitting in a circle holding hands and praying, have them think of how God loves them and makes them feel loved.

SS1825

Rejoicing! Rooms

(children draw themselves in rooms, praying)

"Pray to the Lord."
Jer. 29:7

"He will show you a large upper room." Mark 14:15

"Yet always rejoicing."
2 Cor. 6:10

"WHEN YOU PRAY, GO INTO YOUR ROOM." Matthew 6:6

Dollhouse furniture, trees, rocks

(cardboard boxes to make "rooms")

A bulletin board depicting REJOICING! ROOMS helps children see there are many places to pray. The children can draw their own rooms, cutting out pictures of furniture and pasting them onto 9″ × 12″ paper. There are other rooms to pray in, too, and the children can make pictures of any room they choose—including outdoor settings.

TABLE ACTIVITY: Have dollhouse furniture, cardboard boxes, and small plastic people for the children to arrange in different rooms.

EXTENDED ACTIVITY: Send a message home suggesting that each family member find a special place where he can pray for twenty minutes, uninterrupted. Later, the family can share their experiences.

Shining Star Publications, Copyright © 1987, A division of Good Apple, Inc.

SS1825

"I WILL BE WITH YOU ALWAYS." Matthew 28:20

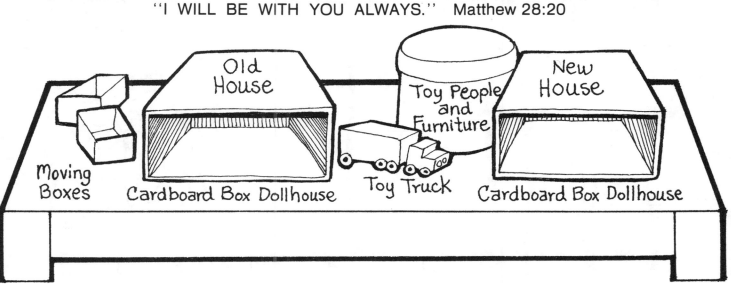

Jesus will be the friend of sad and lonely children. The illustration of a child alone will help children to see the real meaning of this verse.

TABLE ACTIVITY: Have a paper doll family move from an old house to a new one (cardboard box houses). See the patterns found on the following page.

Who is the friend of the family in the new house, before they meet the new neighbors? (And after, of course!)

SS1825

WHO WILL BE MY FRIEND?
(Patterns)
(Family to "move" from old house to new house)

fold back to stand

fold back to stand

SS1825

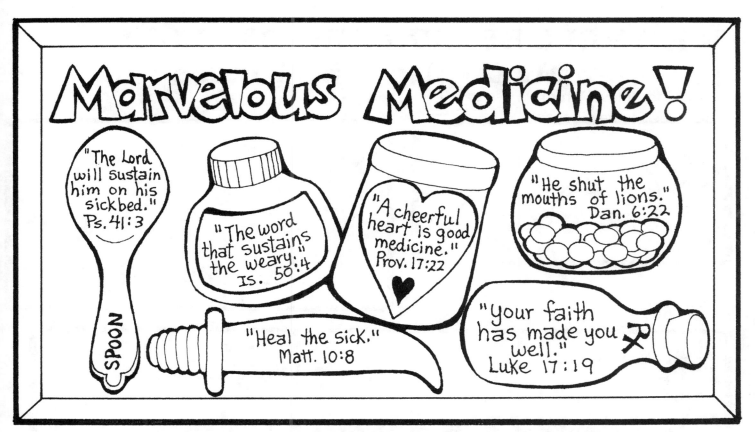

Marvelous Medicine!

"The Lord will sustain him on his sickbed." Ps. 41:3

SPOON

"The word that sustains the weary." Is. 50:4

"A cheerful heart is good medicine." Prov. 17:22

"He shut the mouths of lions." Dan. 6:22

"Heal the sick." Matt. 10:8

"Your faith has made you well." Luke 17:19

"RESTORE HIM FROM HIS BED OF ILLNESS." Psalm 41:3

Graffiti by children

Visit from a friend

Special food

A book to read

A phone call

WHAT CHEERS YOU UP WHEN YOU ARE FEELING SICK?

MARVELOUS MEDICINE! helps children begin to realize how spiritual thoughts and actions can help keep them happy and healthy, and ministers to those who are sick. The teacher (or children) make "medicine" bottles to decorate with verses (see next page). The teacher makes the caption.

(The verses are to be read to the young child; they are not intended for memorization.)

The graffiti on the table, created by the children, shows how they can put some of the thoughts into action. What cheers them up when they are sick? What could they do for others? The teacher will have to write a sentence by each picture, to explain the child's idea.

EXTENDED ACTIVITY: Make small favors for dinner trays for a nursing home, and write short letters or draw pictures for their grandparents.

SS1825

VERSES FOR "MARVELOUS MEDICINE" BOTTLES

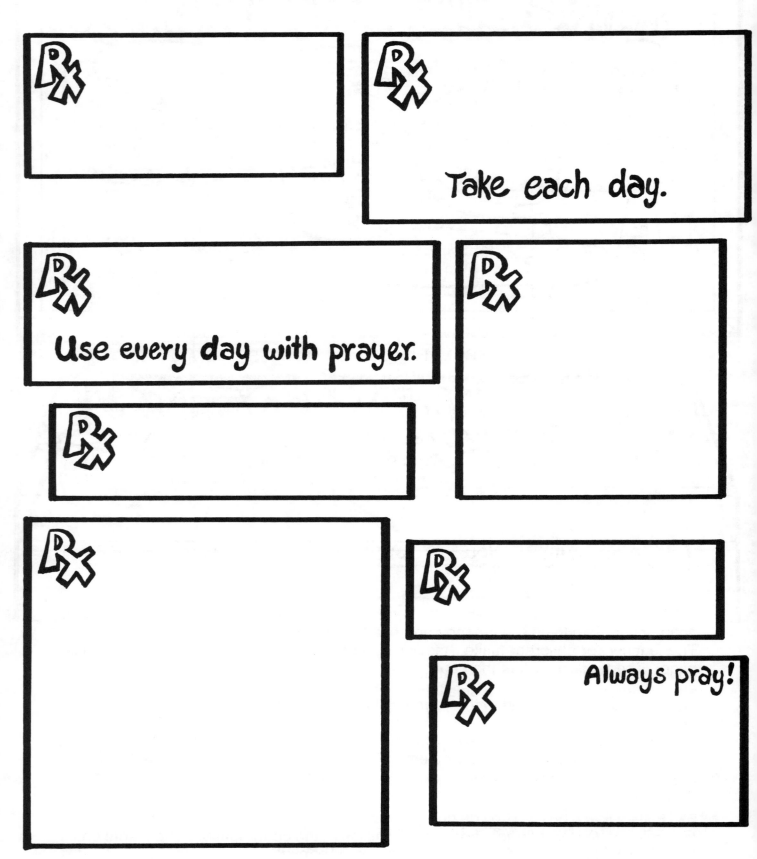

Take each day.

Use every day with prayer.

Always pray!

SS1825

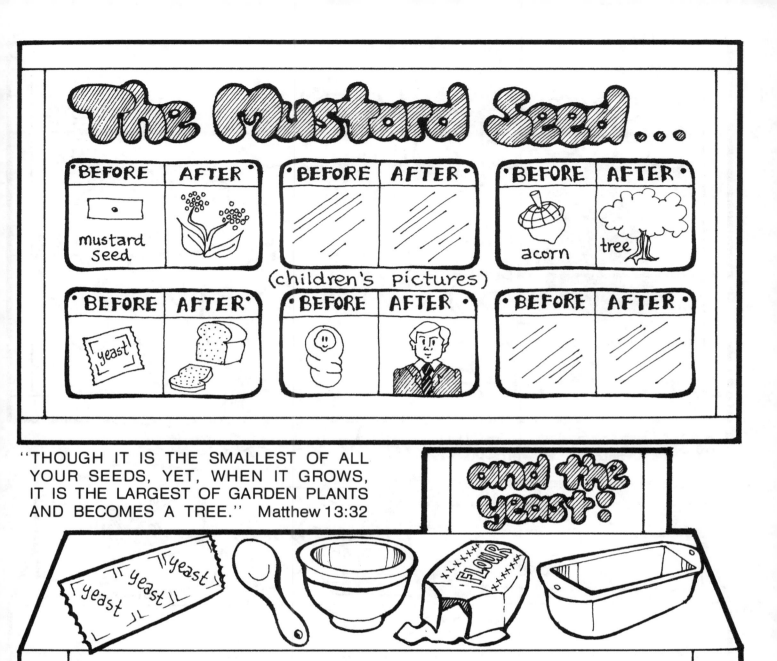

The Mustard Seed...

BEFORE	AFTER
mustard seed	

BEFORE	AFTER

BEFORE	AFTER
acorn	tree

(children's pictures)

BEFORE	AFTER
yeast	

BEFORE	AFTER

BEFORE	AFTER

"THOUGH IT IS THE SMALLEST OF ALL YOUR SEEDS, YET, WHEN IT GROWS, IT IS THE LARGEST OF GARDEN PLANTS AND BECOMES A TREE." Matthew 13:32

and the yeast!

THE MUSTARD SEED . . . AND THE YEAST! is a two-part activity display, which could begin with a reading of Matthew 13:31-33. The children can make before and after pictures showing how a small thing can grow and grow—like Heaven, as explained by Jesus.

TABLE ACTIVITY: Use yeast to make dough rise, and bake bread if time permits. The children could at least see the dough begin to rise, in a one-hour class. This will help them understand the concept of growth.

EXTENDED ACTIVITY: Provide cuttings from several plants. Let the children root the cuttings and then send them home with families in the congregation. The plants could be shared again and again, due to the children's efforts.

SS1825

FOOTPRINTS shows Jesus as the director of lives, as a director directs a play. Jesus is shown sitting in a director's chair, holding a Bible. Students trace one another's feet, cut them out, and pin on the display.

TABLE ACTIVITY: Make dioramas with shoe boxes, paper, scissors and glue. Children can make scenes from lives directed by the Lord Jesus.

People and items for the display can be drawn on triangles of paper, as shown, so that they will stand.

SS1825

And the Walls Come a Tumblin' Down!

(Tape)

"Advance! March around the city."
Josh. 6:7

(Construction paper brick wall made by children)

"BY FAITH THE WALLS OF JERICHO FELL." Hebrews 11:30

Tape

Sun   Moon   Wall of blocks   Red paper to make bricks for display

AND THE WALLS COME A TUMBLIN' DOWN! This bulletin board contains a caption and a trumpet, both made by the teacher. The children can tear the red construction paper into "bricks" to add to the display.

TABLE ACTIVITY: Build a walled city with playing blocks. The children march around the city when the sun is held up by one child and pretend to sleep when another child holds up the moon. The sun is held up seven times, the moon six times. The first six "days" the class marches around the city once. On the seventh day the class marches around the room seven times, blowing imaginary trumpets and then giving a shout. Then one child knocks down the walled city of blocks. ("THEN SHOUT!" Joshua 6:10.) Read Joshua 6:1-11 to the children.

EXTENDED ACTIVITY: Invite another class in to do the marching activity with your class, or perform it for another class. A song to accompany this story will add to the performance.

SS1825

"LET YOUR CONVERSATION BE ALWAYS FULL OF GRACE, SEASONED WITH SALT, SO THAT YOU MAY KNOW HOW TO ANSWER EVERYONE."

Colossians 4:6

YOU ARE THE SALT OF THE EARTH! contains the caption and a large salt shaker made of paper or tagboard. The children cut and tear many faces of people from magazines . . . people of all ages and people from all kinds of places, perhaps doing different things. This collage by the children will help to build an awareness that God's people are everywhere.

TABLE ACTIVITY: Have books about people . . . people farming, people working, people from other countries, and so on, for the children to look at.

EXTENDED ACTIVITY: Have the children make individual collages that might include pictures of themselves, as take-home projects. ANOTHER EXTENDED ACTIVITY would be to listen to the song from *Godspell*, "Light of the World." Perhaps part of the church choir would make a guest appearance to sing this song!

SS1825

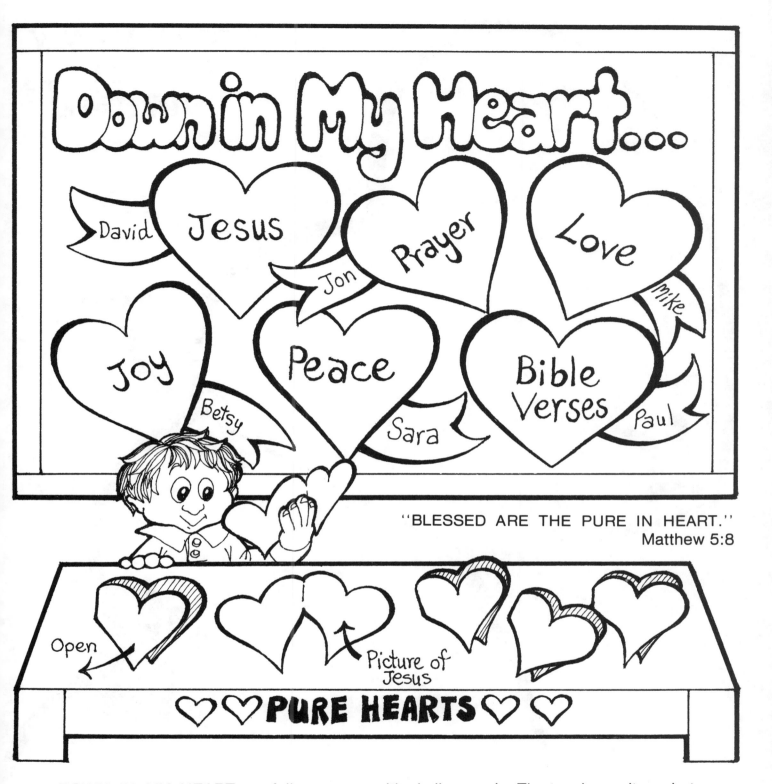

"BLESSED ARE THE PURE IN HEART."
Matthew 5:8

DOWN IN MY HEART can follow a song with similar words. The teacher writes what each child wants "down" in his heart, then puts the child's name on a ribbon attached to the heart.

"GOD, WHO COMFORTS THE DOWNCAST." II Corinthians 7:6

"Pure Hearts" are to be made for the TABLE ACTIVITY. The students can illustrate the insides of the hearts and share with each other. (See pattern found on the following page.)

"THE LORD SEARCHES EVERY HEART." I Chronicles 28:9

SS1825

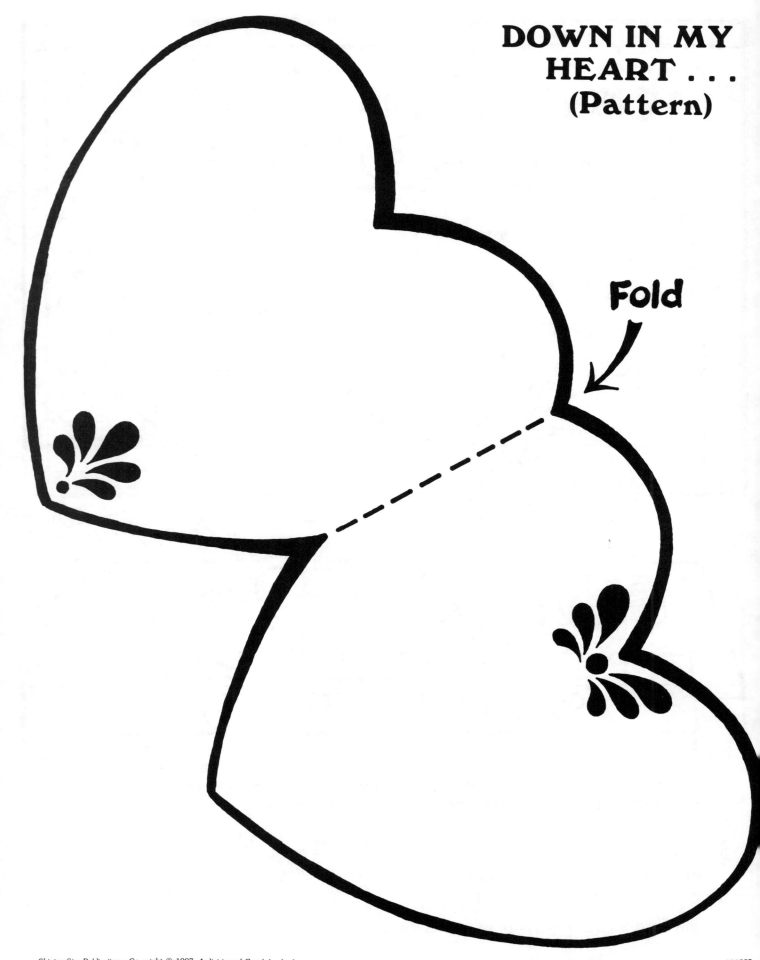

DOWN IN MY HEART . . .
(Pattern)

Fold

SS1825

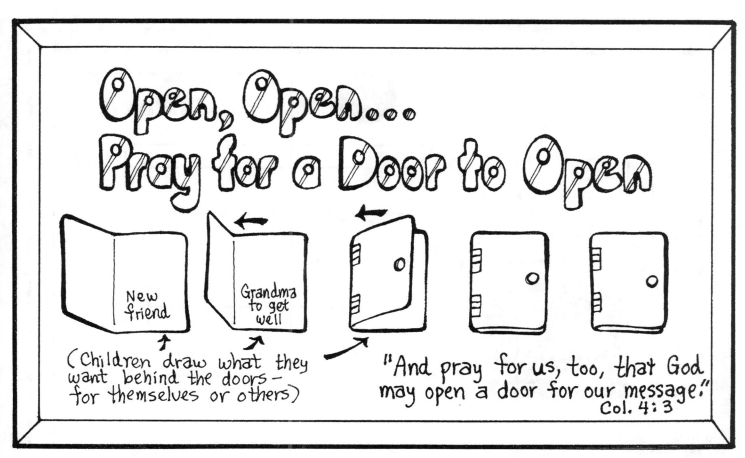

"AND THE DOOR WILL BE OPENED TO YOU." Matthew 7:7

OPEN, OPEN . . . PRAY FOR A DOOR TO OPEN will help children visualize what they hear adults talking about when praying for a door to open. Have children illustrate their prayers in the space provided on the patterns. The teacher may print the idea being conveyed by each child. (See following page for pattern.) Display the completed doors as shown, by pinning the back side to the bulletin board and leaving the "door" part free to swing open.

TABLE ACTIVITY: The children should have picture prayer books to look at and think about.

EXTENDED ACTIVITY: Have an older class come in and read the little prayer books to the children, individually or in small groups.

SS1825

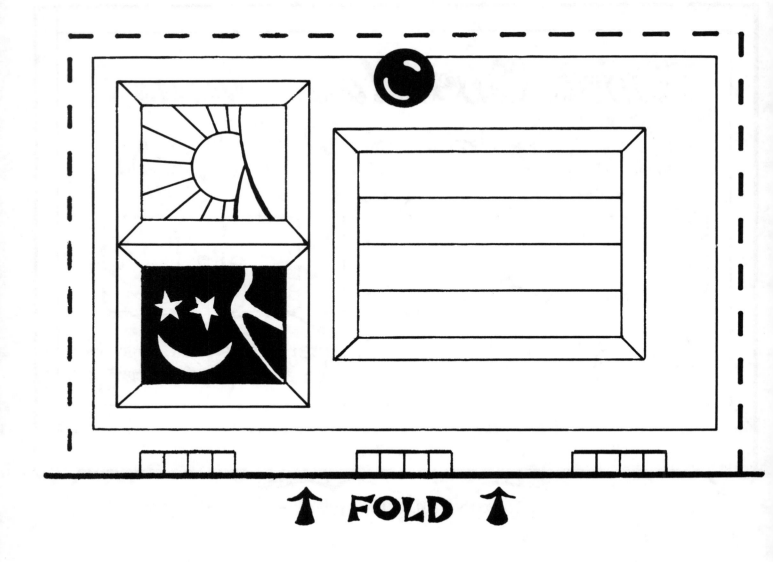

↑ FOLD ↑

(Draw picture on back side of this half-page.
It will be displayed when the door is opened.

SS1825

Happy Birthday, Jesus!
December 25th

"So they hurried off and found Mary and Joseph, and the baby."
Luke 2:16

(Children design presents for Jesus)

"YOU WILL FIND A BABY WRAPPED IN CLOTHS AND LYING IN A MANGER."
Luke 2:12

Paper

Scissors

Pencils

Crayons

HAPPY BIRTHDAY, JESUS! needs a caption and verses prepared by the teacher. The children draw, color, cut and display the gifts they would like to give Jesus.

TABLE ACTIVITY: Have materials for making Christmas cards. The children can make them to give to others to tell about the birth of Jesus. (Birth announcements.)

EXTENDED ACTIVITY: Have someone from the congregation dress up as Jesus and receive the gifts when the display is taken down.

SS1825

The OBEY BAY display contains a bay with boats. On each boat is printed a verse about obeying. You may use plastic boats, writing on them with a permanent marker.

TABLE ACTIVITY: Have two pans of water. Students might be allowed to play with the boats and water as a reward for memorizing the Scriptures. A box of things to experiment with could be provided for students to see what will and won't float.

Towels will be helpful!

SS1825

HELPERS IN OUR CHURCH

Pastor Secretary Custodian Elder ← Photos

Kitchen Helper Usher (etc.)

"AND SOME TO BE PASTORS AND TEACHERS, TO PREPARE GOD'S PEOPLE FOR WORKS OF SERVICE . . . TO THE WHOLE MEASURE OF THE FULLNESS OF CHRIST."

Ephesians 4:11-13

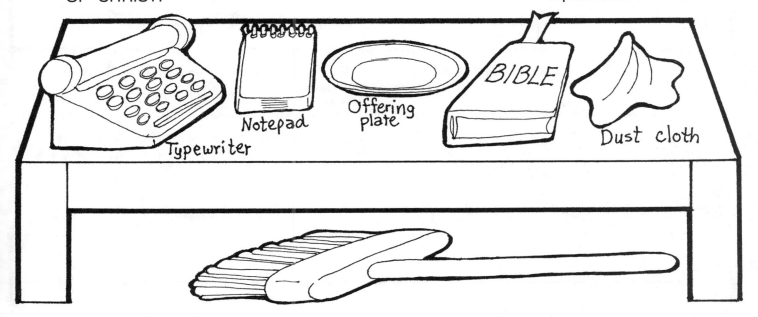

The HELPERS IN OUR CHURCH display is intended to broaden the children's awareness of how many people it takes to run a church. Each church helper could come in for a five-minute interview. A drawing or photo of each class visitor could be displayed on the bulletin board.

TABLE ACTIVITY: Have some of the tools the different people use in their jobs. A toy typewriter, a broom, and so on, might be useful. The items might be brought in by those interviewed.

EXTENDED ACTIVITY: Take a tour of the church and see where the different people work. Note the items talked about and where they are located.

SS1825

"You must not eat from the tree..."

Gen. 2:17

Have no other Gods

Do not be unfaithful

Do not steal

Do not misuse God's name

Do not murder

Do not covet other things

Do not lie about a neighbor

Do not covet your neighbor's house

Keep Sunday holy

Honor your mother and father

"A NEW COMMAND I GIVE YOU: LOVE ONE ANOTHER. AS I HAVE LOVED YOU, SO YOU MUST LOVE ONE ANOTHER." John 13:34

Bad apple

Bad apple cut open

YOU MUST NOT EAT FROM THE TREE will help preschool children begin to understand what the Ten Commandments are all about. They don't need to memorize them, or even to understand them all; but some awareness is possible, even for very young children. The eight commandments that are "do nots" are represented as bad apples hanging on a tree. (Compare it to the one in the Garden of Eden.) The other commandments about things that we *should* do are put on other trees.

TABLE ACTIVITY: Have a bowl of apples containing one or two bad ones among the good. The teacher can show the inside of a rotten apple by cutting it open and comparing it to how badly we would feel if we broke a commandment.

SS1825

"INDEED, THE VERY HAIRS OF YOUR HEAD ARE ALL NUMBERED."
Luke 12:7

HAIRY HEADS! provides a source of wonderment and awe for the children. Ask them how many hairs are on their heads. Try to count one child's hairs! After the teacher makes the caption and pins up the verses, the children can draw pictures of themselves, using real yarn for hair. Did they use as many pieces of yarn as the number of real hairs they have?

TABLE ACTIVITY: Comb and brush a doll's hair, taking time to wonder how God can know how many hairs every person has . . . What else might God know? (How many stars there are, etc.) Can they count the hairs on one doll's head?

EXTENDED ACTIVITY: Have a circle discussion and name other things they think God might know. Read aloud Matthew 10:29-31. What things might God care about? (sparrows, people, etc.)

SS1825

PRAISE HIM WITH THE STRINGS AND FLUTE. (Psalm 150:4) Pictures of musical instruments may be displayed, or students may construct simple instruments by stretching rubber bands over box lids, making flutes from paper dowels, etc.

A rhythm band could be formed for a praise parade. Children could march around the room while the piano or a record is played.

SS1825

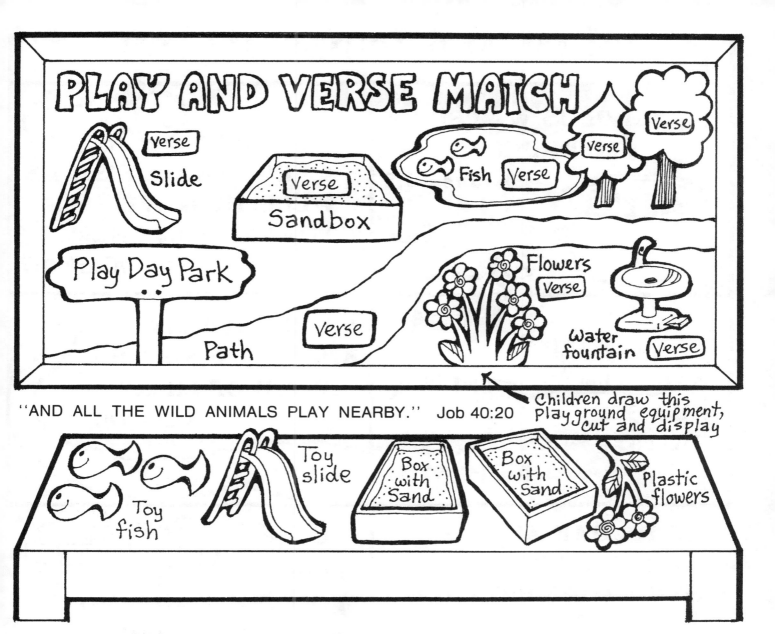

PLAY AND VERSE MATCH

Verse

Slide

Verse

Sandbox

Fish Verse

Verse

Verse

Play Day Park

Flowers

Verse

Verse

Path

Water fountain

Verse

Children draw this playground equipment, cut and display

"AND ALL THE WILD ANIMALS PLAY NEARBY."   Job 40:20

Toy fish

Toy slide

Box with Sand

Box with Sand

Plastic flowers

In the PLAY AND VERSE MATCH! display the children contribute the playground equipment. They can color, cut and pin their portion of the bulletin board. The teacher contributes the caption and the printed verses. (See following page.)

After the children have finished their creations and have displayed them, the teacher reads the verses and asks the children where each should be pinned. Example—"GIVE US WATER TO DRINK" Exodus 17:2 should be placed near the fountain. These verses are intended to show the variety of verses in the Bible, and are not for student memorization.

Sand in cardboard box lids

EXTENDED ACTIVITY: Do finger drawing in sandbox.

SS1825

PLAY AND VERSE MATCH

"GIVE US WATER TO DRINK."
Exodus 17:2

"THEY HAD  A FEW SMALL FISH AS WELL: HE GAVE THANKS FOR THEM."
Mark 8:7

"HIS FEET DO NOT SLIP."
Psalm 37:31

"YOU HAVE MADE KNOWN TO ME THE PATH OF LIFE."
Psalm 16:11

"SO HE RAN AHEAD AND CLIMBED A SYCAMORE-FIG TREE."
Luke 19:4

"LIKE A FOOLISH MAN WHO BUILT HIS HOUSE ON SAND."
Matthew 7:26

"LIKE A FLOWER OF THE FIELD."
Psalm 103:15

"THE PINE, THE FIR, AND THE CYPRESS TOGETHER."
Isaiah 60:13

SS1825

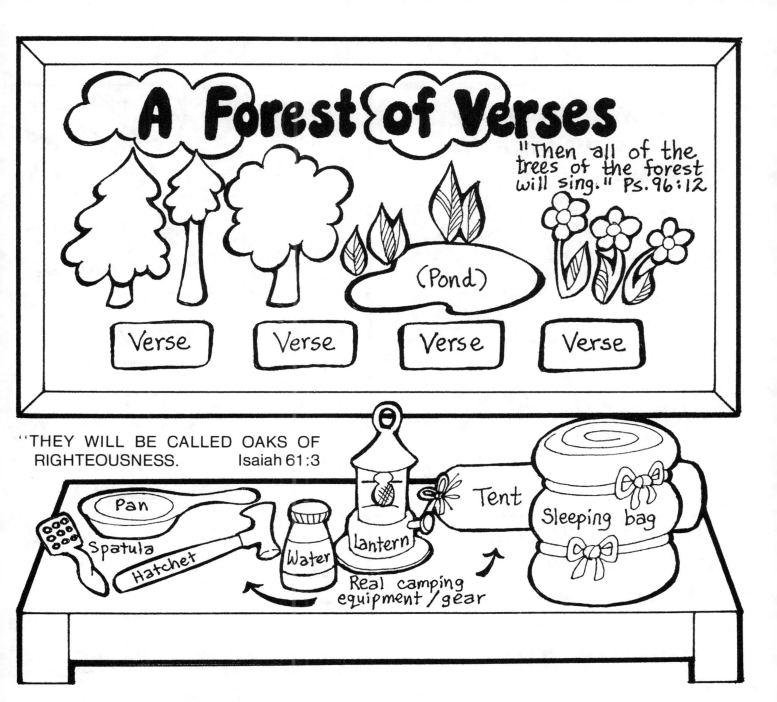

In A FOREST OF VERSES the children help create flowers, trees, clouds, and other forest items to pin on the bulletin board.

The teacher prepares the caption and the verses to add to the display. The verses on the following page can be cut apart and used for that purpose. The verses are not intended for student memorization—only for awareness.

TABLE ACTIVITY: Have children bring camping gear from home. The children could snuggle in their sleeping bags while the teacher reads some Bible stories. The children could say their prayers and pretend to sleep. This might be done to build interest for an upcoming church camping experience.

EXTENDED ACTIVITY: A church camp-out weekend would really be an extended activity!

SS1825

A FOREST OF VERSES

"THE WILDERNESS WILL REJOICE AND BLOSSOM."

Isaiah 35:1

"BIRDS OF EVERY KIND WILL NEST IN IT; THEY WILL FIND SHELTER IN THE SHADE OF ITS BRANCHES."

Ezekiel 17:23

"HE MAKES THE CLOUDS HIS CHARIOT AND RIDES ON THE WINGS OF THE WIND."   Psalm 104:3

"LIKE A TREE PLANTED BY STREAMS OF WATER."

Psalm 1:3

SS1825

At the end of our Rainbow...

(Children draw things to put in pot for end of rainbow)

BIBLE

"THIS IS THE SIGN OF THE COVENANT I AM MAKING BETWEEN ME AND YOU."
Genesis 9:12

(Paint)

(Brushes)

(Paper for objects and painting rainbows)

"I HAVE SET MY RAINBOW IN THE CLOUDS."   Genesis 9:13

What would be at the end of a rainbow of true happiness? Gold, perhaps, but encourage children to think of what really makes a happy life. The teacher arranges the display of rainbow streams of color and an empty pot. The children then color, cut, and pin on objects at the end of the rainbow.

TABLE ACTIVITY: Paint rainbows and mix colors to make "new" colors. Encourage the children to clean up carefully after painting.

EXTENDED ACTIVITY: Paint a rainbow on a window of the church for everyone to enjoy.

"I have set my rainbow in the clouds." Gen. 9:13

SS1825

"TRUST IN THE LORD AND DO GOOD." Psalm 37:3
"ON TOWARD LOVE AND GOOD DEEDS." Hebrews 10:24

This display focuses on doors . . . KNOCK, KNOCK,
WHO'S THERE?
PEOPLE IN OUR CHURCH WHO CARE!

The tagboard doors open and reveal things families do to help make sure the church functions. Students could cut and paste pictures or draw pictures to go behind the doors: someone raking leaves, teaching a class, collecting the offering.

What do the students already know about how people help the church? What did they learn? What do the students do to help the church? What will they do for the church when they grow up?

EXTENDED ACTIVITY: Have students interview church members and find out what they do to help the church.

SS1825

TIME TO TRUST helps children understand being in touch with God. A calendar, an old watch, a paper-plate clock (pattern follows), and pages from a date book give the children some concrete time measures. All the days, all the hours—always—we can trust and love God.

TABLE ACTIVITY: Display some time-related things, such as toys or nonworking clocks and watches, calendars and datebooks. The children can find important dates on the calendar—birthdays, Christmas, etc. Would they trust in the Lord those days?

EXTENDED ACTIVITY: Make a paper-plate clock with hands that have words printed on them: "Trust in Him . . . Always." (See next page for clock face pattern.) Copy the pattern, cut out, and paste onto a paper plate.

SS1825

TIME TO TRUST . . . ACTIVITY PAGE
(Pattern)

use on paper plate

"Trust in Him at all times."
Ps. 62:8

TRUST IN HIM

ALWAYS

Cut out hands and attach to paper plate with brass fastener.

SS1825

Noise and Rejoice!

LOUD!

"Shout for joy to the Lord, all the earth." Ps. 98:4

"He leads me beside quiet waters." Ps. 23:2

SOFT

"HE WILL QUIET YOU WITH HIS LOVE."   Zephaniah 3:17

Band instruments (for shouting with joy)

Bible stories (for quiet rejoicing)

"BURST INTO SONG, O MOUNTAINS!" Isaiah 49:13

"IN QUIETNESS AND TRUST IS YOUR STRENGTH." Isaiah 30:15

NOISE AND REJOICE concentrates on the sounds of rejoicing. A joyful person shouts for joy on one side of the display, while the other side shows a quiet person.

TABLE ACTIVITY: Display toy band instruments for singing and shouting for joy; quieter moments can be shared with Bible story books.

The teacher rings a bell once and students use the noisy instruments; two rings from the bell means to look quietly at a book. The students will enjoy going back and forth between loud and quiet activities.

SS1825

Star Splendor

"Star differs from star in splendor."   I Cor. 15:41

Stars made by children, with some made of foil.

(Black background)

"THE SUN HAS ONE KIND OF SPLENDOR, THE MOON ANOTHER AND THE STARS ANOTHER."   I Corinthians 15:41

① Paper Crayons Bobby pins

② Blue paint Brushes

"MY LOVE TO ALL OF YOU IN JESUS CHRIST."   I Corinthians 16:24

STAR SPLENDOR will help children see that people are unique and that they shine in different areas. Children can make stars of foil or paper to add to the black paper background.

TABLE ACTIVITY: Instruct each child to draw a rainbow, using pressure on the crayon as he draws. When the rainbow is complete, have the child color over the entire picture with black crayon. A bobby pin can be used to etch stars. A student can also draw stars on a blank page, cover the picture with blue water paint and let the stars shine through.

SS1825

Who is...
the Greatest in the Kingdom of Heaven?
Matt. 18:1

(Answers coming next week!)

Guesses Here

"I TELL YOU THE TRUTH, UNLESS YOU CHANGE AND BECOME LIKE LITTLE CHILDREN, YOU WILL NEVER ENTER THE KINGDOM OF HEAVEN."
Matthew 18:3

Magazine pictures of people likely to be great in Heaven

Paper for guesses

WHO IS . . . THE GREATEST IN THE KINGDOM OF HEAVEN? is a question the children can respond to by selecting pictures or writing guesses on slips of paper. The guesses can be added to the bag in the display. Use discussion.

TABLE ACTIVITY: Have the children select pictures from magazines of who they think is likely to be great in Heaven. Discussions will develop among children about selections.

Next week, repeat Matthew 18:3 and talk to your students about children entering the Kingdom of Heaven. Display several magazine pictures of children.

SS1825

"HEAVEN IS LIKE A NET."
Matthew 13:47

This bulletin board entitled NEW NETS emphasizes Bible verses which include the word NEW. How many names can be caught in nets by children who memorize the verses?

TABLE ACTIVITY: Have a small net with a pan of water. Floating ducks might have verses written on their bottoms with permanent marker. A student can try to catch the duck with the verse he/she can say aloud.

SS1825

For Our Church...

Silver — and — Gold

Reversible Coins and Currency (coin on front— picture on back)

What do they do?

This 1¢ helps buy paper. (etc.)

"ABRAM HAD BECOME VERY WEALTHY IN LIVESTOCK AND IN SILVER AND GOLD."

Genesis 13:2

Items to let children pretend to send bills and pay bills for church → Play money

Play cash register   Calculator

Pretend bills

Receipts

Bill paying envelopes

In this display, SILVER AND GOLD, WHAT DO THEY DO? the children become familiar with the ways money is used to help run a church and missions. Large "coins" of tagboard are cut out and different monetary amounts are written on one side of each. On the other side are pasted pictures of different ways the money could be used to help the church. These pictures might come from church magazines or from illustrations drawn by older students. The coins can be reversed during discussion.

TABLE ACTIVITY: Have paper money and play cash registers. The children might write out play "bills" and send them to the church "office" for payment with play money.

> "LEAVE YOUR GIFT
> THERE IN FRONT OF
> THE ALTAR."
> Matthew 5:24

SS1825

"A WORD APTLY SPOKEN IS LIKE APPLES OF GOLD IN SETTINGS OF SILVER."
Proverbs 25:11

The APPLES OF GOLD display is made by fastening gold paper apples to a silver foil background. The apples should be blank when students arrive in class. During a class discussion, write polite things to say to each other on the apples.

Apple bobbing would be a memorable and fun way to reinforce Proverbs 25:11.

SS1825

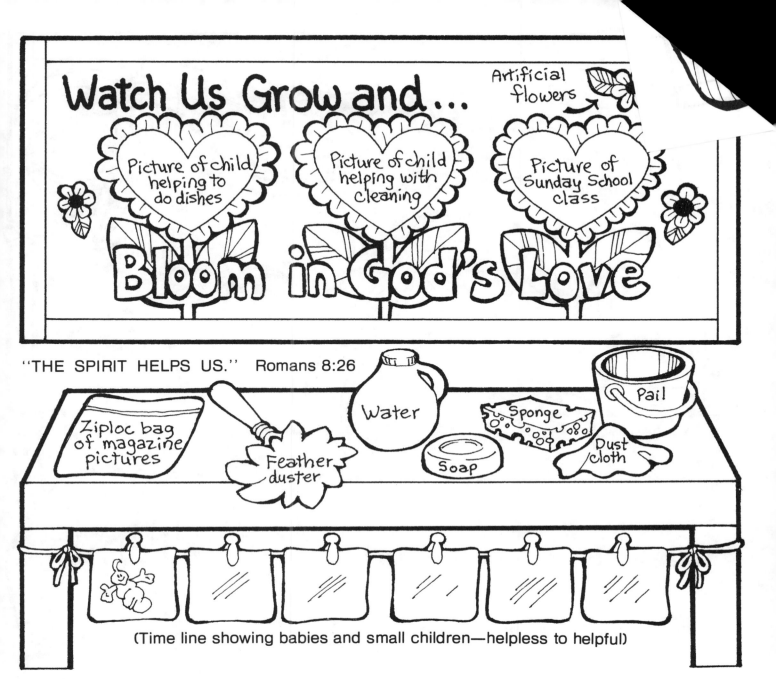

Watch Us Grow and...

Artificial flowers

Picture of child helping to do dishes

Picture of child helping with cleaning

Picture of Sunday School class

Bloom in God's Love

"THE SPIRIT HELPS US." Romans 8:26

Ziploc bag of magazine pictures

Feather duster

Water

Soap

Sponge

Pail

Dust cloth

(Time line showing babies and small children—helpless to helpful)

For the display BLOOM IN GOD'S LOVE, use pictures of the children being helpful at home. Ask the children how they have grown from being helpless to being helpful.

(NOTE: The poem on the following page, "Watch Us Grow," can be reproduced and a copy given to each child to color and take home.)

TABLE ACTIVITY: Have some cleaning supplies (safe items) for children to use in the classroom to demonstrate their helpfulness.

Use clothespins to put up a time line of pictures from a family magazine. The children could arrange the pictures from the most helpless to the most helpful.

EXTENDED ACTIVITY: Help clean a closet or another classroom—such as the nursery, after use—for the church.

SS1825

WATCH US GROW!

We are the children of our
    God and King.
Jesus was His only Son.
We know that Jesus is the real
    vine,
We are the branches.
He loves everyone.
And watch us grow, watch us grow,
    watch us grow
To where we care and share and give.

Help us grow, help us grow, help us grow
To be like Jesus.
He's the one who helps us to live.

Jackie Bell

SS1825

IT'S PLANTING TIME! Six different kinds of seeds are started in a pot on the table at the bottom of the bulletin board. Small stakes are placed near each planting, a string is attached to each one, and a label with the plant name is added. After the seeds germinate, the students match the plants with the packages of seeds which have been pinned onto the bulletin board.

EXTENDED ACTIVITY: Plant seeds so that the children will have plants to give as Mother's Day and shut-in gifts.

> **"THERE IS A TIME FOR EVERYTHING."**
> **Ecclesiastes 3:1**

SS1825

BEARING BANNERS

"His banner over me is love." Song 2:4

"Bearing with one another in love." Eph. 4:2

LOVE

"THE LORD IS MY BANNER."
Exodus 17:15

Banner supplies

(Burlap on small dowels with yarn)

(Felt to cut and paste)

BEARING BANNERS provides an opportunity for the children to make burlap banners. A banner-like display with the word LOVE would help students think about the verse, "HIS BANNER OVER ME IS LOVE." Song of Solomon 2:4

Small banners could be made by the children with burlap, small dowels, and felt. This could be done in conjunction with any Sunday School lesson.

EXTENDED ACTIVITY: Have children take their banners to shut-ins as gifts of love.

Shining Star Publications, Copyright © 1987, A division of Good Apple, Inc.

SS1825

Silent Secrets

What Does Our Father in Heaven Want Us to Do in Secret?

Pray — Matt. 6:5-8

Give to the needy — Matt. 6:1-4

Soothe anger — Prov. 21:14

Keep a secret — Prov. 11:13

Be silent — Eccles. 3:7

"THEN YOUR FATHER, WHO SEES WHAT IS DONE IN SECRET, WILL REWARD YOU."
Matthew 6:6

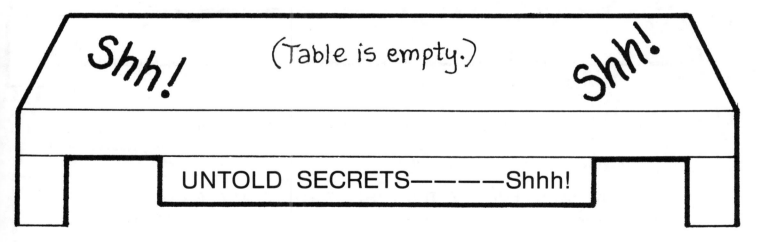

Shh!   (Table is empty.)   Shh!

UNTOLD SECRETS—————Shhh!

In this display, SILENT SECRETS, the lesson to the children is that giving and prayer may sometimes be done in secret. God will know and reward; the secret is between the child and God. Each child should draw a picture of a "silent secret" he could do sometime. The teacher provides a scriptural caption for each picture.

TABLE ACTIVITY: The table is left empty to emphazise the concept being taught.

EXTENDED ACTIVITY: Encourage each child to do a good deed, in secret, during the next few days.

SS1825

"I HAVE THE DESIRE TO DO WHAT IS GOOD."   Romans 7:18

"HOW BEAUTIFUL ARE THE FEET OF THOSE WHO BRING GOOD NEWS."
Romans 10:15

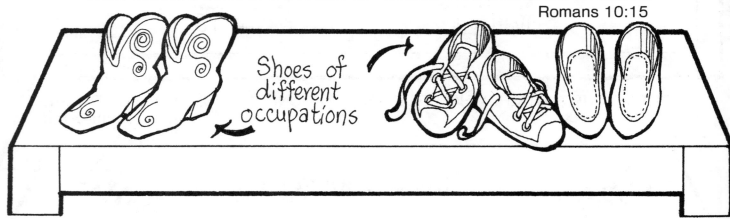

FLEET FEET asks what good news the children would like to share. That they love Christ? That church is nice? That God loves everyone? The feet of the children with such thoughts as these are beautiful.

> "HOW BEAUTIFUL ARE THE FEET OF THOSE WHO BRING GOOD NEWS."   Romans 10:15

The children could be shown a Good News Bible and told that it shares the really good news of God's love.

The children can trace and cut out outlines of their own feet to pin to the display. They might glue sequins and other shiny things to these very beautiful feet for a really eye-catching display!!

EXTENDED ACTIVITY: Place the shoes of different occupations on the table. Allow time for children to try to identify the occupation of the person that would wear each pair of shoes. Examples: ballet slippers, fireman's boots, etc.

SS1825

UNIQUE! emphasizes to the children that each person is special and different from others, as each and every snowflake is unique. The children cut out snowflakes (circles folded in half, then into three sections, so they have six points). The teacher makes the caption for this display.

TABLE ACTIVITY: Have flat pieces of cardboard or empty cardboard boxes wrapped and tied with ribbon, so that they resemble gifts. A different fruit of the Spirit should be written on each package, in preparation for discussion of this verse:

"BUT THE FRUIT OF THE SPIRIT IS LOVE, JOY, PEACE, PATIENCE, KINDNESS, GOODNESS, FAITHFULNESS, GENTLENESS, AND SELF-CONTROL." Galatians 5:22,23

The children can play giving these "gifts" to their dolls, each other, etc.

SS1825

Forget Me Not...

"May He turn our hearts to Him."
I Kings 8:58

"LIKEWISE, EVERY GOOD TREE BEARS GOOD FRUIT."
Matthew 7:17

"DO NOT FORGET THE LORD."
Deuteronomy 6:12

FORGET ME NOT . . . .

This display requires the caption and the hand pattern. Students design their own cuffs and draw on the hands what they will do to remember the Lord.

See if they can remember the verses, as well!

EXTENDED ACTIVITY: Use the hand pattern as an award each time a child memorizes a Bible verse. Write the caption "I remember" on the hand and the Scripture reference for the verse memorized on the cuff.

Decorate your own cuff

"And do not forget to do good." Heb. 13:16

SS1825

"HIS HEART IS STEADFAST, TRUSTING IN THE LORD." Psalm 112:7, is a display that gives children some idea about constant and steadfast love. Ask the children how they would describe this kind of love.

TABLE ACTIVITY: Have cutout hearts for the children to look at. Some of them could be made by the teacher, some by the children. The hearts could be used in play by the children and also in a circle prayer. The teacher could have the children hold up their hearts and say, "We thank you, Lord, for love—which Cindy is holding . . ." and the children would respond with, "We thank you, Lord, for love." Continue around the circle until every child has had a turn.

SS1825

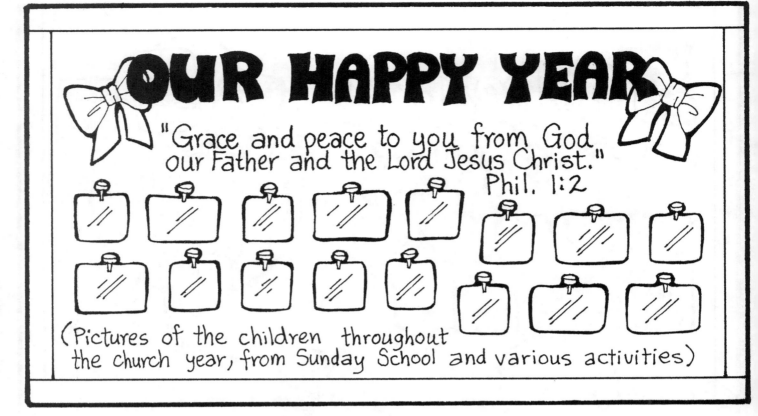

"I THANK MY GOD EVERY TIME I REMEMBER YOU." Philippians 1:3

(Odds and ends – extras of lessons from the year)

This display, OUR HAPPY YEAR, would help wrap up the Sunday School year, with photos of the children in class and at various church activities.

TABLE ACTIVITY: The children could complete leftover lesson pages from the year in their spare time.

Perhaps the teacher could write this verse on small hand-decorated index cards, to give to the children on the last class day:

"I THANK MY GOD EVERY TIME I REMEMBER YOU."
Philippians 1:3

EXTENDED ACTIVITY: Put scrapbooks of the past year's highlights on the table for children to enjoy. Include some of their own photographs, which they can bring from home.

SS1825

"ON TOWARD LOVE AND GOOD DEEDS." Hebrews 10:24

The SEEDS OF GOOD DEEDS display begins with a discussion of what kind of person does good deeds. What would we like about that person? The children can be given copies of seed packages (see following page) to decorate and display. The teacher will have to write the word of the "seed," such as *helpfulness, kindness, joy*, and so on. (A child may mention "not hitting my brother." This is valid for a child!)

EXTENDED ACTIVITY: Have each child invent a new flower. Have him name the flower, draw a picture of it, and list its qualities on the seed packages found on the following page.

SS1825

SEEDS OF GOOD DEEDS
ACTIVITY PAGE

SS1825

Finding a Book in the Bible...

ACTS

37   6

10

ACTS

7   31

20

ACTS

for Young Learners

① Open Bible
② Look at darker words at top of page.
③ Look until you match a book and the word you selected.

"AND THE BOOKS WERE OPENED."   Daniel 7:10

Bookmarkers

FINDING A BOOK IN THE BIBLE demonstrates the first step in learning to locate a chapter, verse or book in the Bible. (See following page, "A Young Learner Story . . . for learning to use the Bible.")

The teacher makes markers for a **few** of the books of the Bible. The teacher shows how to locate a Bible book and hands out markers for the children to use. The activity is easy to check and requires no real reading—just matching a few letters in the word. Encourage and help the children.

After children can identify a book in the Bible, the chapter number can be added, followed by the verse number.

No reading by the children is needed. The teacher can read a few Bible verses aloud.

Shining Star Publications, Copyright © 1987, A division of Good Apple, Inc.   SS1825

A Young Learner story...
for learning to use the Bible...

How I Found a Book in the Bible!

NAME _____

•Story One

I found my Bible and my word marker...

①

I looked and looked until I found an "A" word at the top of the page...

(It had to be an "A" word with a "t" in it...) ②

I marked my place when I found Acts,

and showed it to my teacher:

Teacher's Signature _____

Date _____

"Learn from me." Matt. 11:29 ③

SS1825

pure and lovely thoughts

"Whatever is true, whatever is pure, whatever is lovely...think about such things."
Phil. 4:8

"AND THE GOD OF PEACE WILL BE WITH YOU." Philippians 4:9

PURE AND LOVELY THOUGHTS can be reflected in the children's silhouettes. Using a lamp to cast a shadow, have the child sit on a chair while the teacher traces his profile on white paper taped to the wall. The child can retrace his profile and focus on pure and lovely thoughts that come to mind, "And the God of peace will be with you."

EXTENDED ACTIVITY: Make another shadow picture of each child, this one black. This silhouette can be framed and sent home for a special day.

SS1825

The Church Is People!

"People served the Lord."
Judg. 2:7

"You are the people of God."
1 Pet. 2:10

"Do as I have done for you."
John 13:15

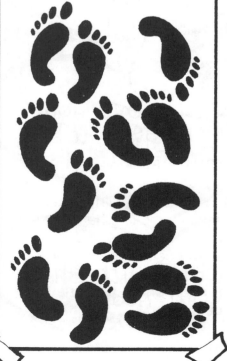

"YOU ARE MY PEOPLE."   Hosea 2:23

Children's hand prints form the shape of a church in this display, THE CHURCH IS PEOPLE! The children place their hands, palms down, in the tempera paint and then press them onto a paper-covered bulletin board.

EXTENDED ACTIVITY: Try a similar approach using children's footprints on a large piece of brown paper leading to a pan of water. The caption "DO AS I HAVE DONE FOR YOU" John 13:15 may be written on the paper near the basin of water.

SS1825

"GOD IS LOVE."   I John 4:8

Use GOD IS LOVE AND FROM ABOVE as the caption. Students can make raindrop hearts to decorate the bulletin board.

Write students' names on hearts when they memorize verses.

EXTENDED ACTIVITY: Encourage children to memorize other verses about love. Write verses on hearts and send home as children memorize.

"That your love may abound more."
Phil. 1:9

"He will love you and bless you."
Deut. 7:13

"God is Love."
I John 4:8

"Love Him with all your heart."
Deut. 13:3

SS1825

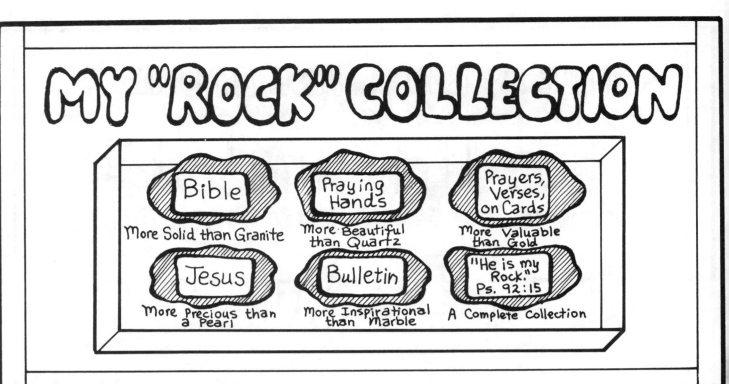

"HE IS MY ROCK."   Psalm 92:15

MY ROCK COLLECTION

This cardboard or tagboard "rock" collection is about the rock which Christ is in our lives. On each cardboard rock is mounted a picture, a prayer or a Bible verse. Labels can describe the value of each item displayed.

EXTENDED ACTIVITY: Paint small smooth rocks with acrylic paints. Symbols of Jesus can be painted on the rocks—shepherd or light, for example.

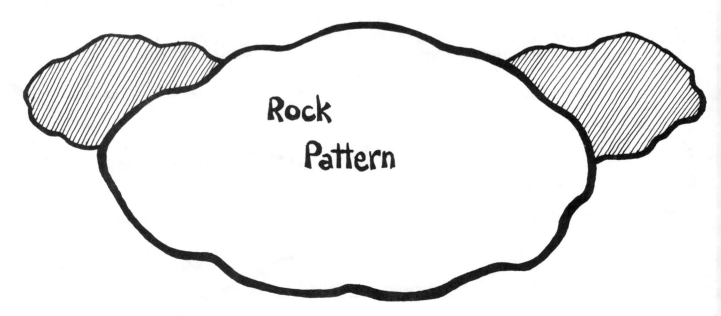

SS1825

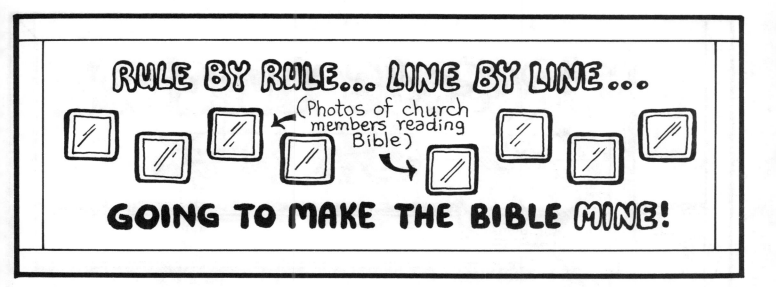

"WISDOM IS MORE PRECIOUS THAN RUBIES."   Proverbs 8:11

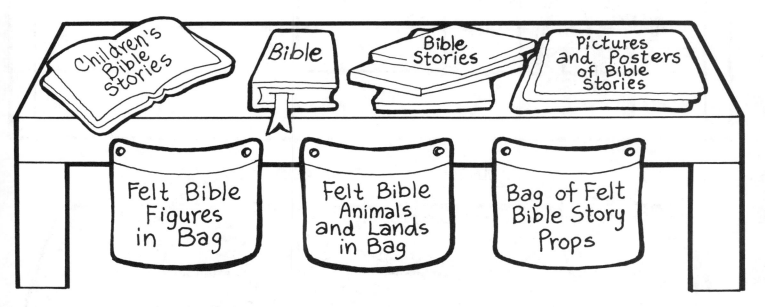

The caption, RULE BY RULE, LINE BY LINE . . . GOING TO MAKE THE BIBLE MINE can be surrounded by pictures of families reading the Bible. Children can bring pictures of their own families reading together.

After children know several Bible stories well, they can dramatize stories using felt figures.

On the table below the display, Bibles, Bible story books and pictures or posters of Bible stories can be placed. The Ziploc bags taped to the table can hold felt Bible figures and other felt props so students can retell the stories.

EXTENDED ACTIVITY: Students who know the stories by heart may use the overhead projector and felt figures to give a shadow story presentation.

"RULE ON RULE . . ."   Isaiah 28:10

SS1825

God's Greatest Gift to Us

Lift

"IF YOU KNEW THE GIFT OF GOD." John 4:10

GOD'S GREATEST GIFT TO US is a bulletin board covered with wrapping paper and ribbon. A portion of the paper is cut so that it can be lifted to reveal a picture of Jesus.

On the table below the display are small wrapped boxes with a student's name on each one. Inside each box is a small picture or sticker of Jesus.

EXTENDED ACTIVITY: Have students wrap packages, each containing a sticker of Jesus. These could be distributed to everyone attending church on a particular Sunday morning.

SS1825

You Were a **Sunbeam** for Jesus Today!

Thank You For: _____

_____

From: _____

Date: _____ Church: _____

You Were a Ray of **Sunshine** in Our Class Today!

To: _____

From: _____

Date: _____ Church: _____

SS1825

Make Music to the Lord

"Let them sing before the Lord,
For He comes to judge the earth."
Ps. 98:9

An Award to: _____

For Singing: _____

Date: _____

Teacher: _____

Church: _____

Glue on gold
star or fill in
star with gold-
paint marker.

A Golden Star For You!

To: _____

From: _____

Reason: _____

_____

Date: _____   Church: _____

SS1825

Angel Award

...for angelic behavior

Church: _____

To: _____
From: _____

_____   _____

Sunbeam Sparkles

You sparkle as a sunbeam for Jesus!

To: _____
From: _____
Church: _____

Use glitter to decorate this award.

SS1825

Well Done!

Glue

1 2 3 4 5 6

THIS AWARD IS PRESENTED TO

_____

for being helpful in Sunday School.

Date: _____
Teacher: _____
Church: _____

"Do and do, do and do, rule on rule, rule
on rule, a little here, a little there."
Is. 28:13

This award can be given with a ruler as a
special gift or award.

Memory Work Award

"This Is a Day of Good News"
2 Kings 7:9

for Bible Memory Work...

Good News

Verses: _____
_____
_____
_____

To: _____
Teacher: _____
Church: _____
Date: _____

SS1825